BUILDING HOPE FOR AMERICA

What We Need To Fix

John Donovan

ISBN-13: 9781234567890
ISBN-10: 1477123456

Cover design by: Art Painter
Library of Congress Control Number: 2018675309
Printed in the United States of America

This book is dedicated to all my black and brown friends. Live a very long time and prosper.

CONTENTS

INTRODUCTION

As the Pandemic rages in America and my staying at home, I have had a lot of time to think about everything that is happening in our country. This is to say there is a lot to fix and question right now. I may not have the answers to all of them, but in most cases I can tell you why it is happening. It is the job of the younger generation to find a cure. Here we go...

THE CONFEDERACY

Living in the south most of my life, this issue has basically two streams of thought. There are those who believe in remembering their relatives. There are also those who honor the Confederacy for its views on the treatment of black people. Let us look at these two issues.

Those who believe in honoring their relatives reminds me of the relatives of Jeffrey Dahmer wanting to honor his memory. I am not sure how many people would like that move on their part. Let us remember that your relatives killed American soldiers. You cannot get around that. No matter how hard you try. As a nation, we have forgotten that. These people cannot be Americans if they honor the Confederacy or their dead relatives who fought this war. Why are we still having this debate in the year 2020? They withdrew from the United States to form a country that was based on White Supremacy. How come the military has allowed Confederate Generals names on military bases. You want to honor the ones who assisted in killing American Soldiers? I think if you put it to a vote in this country about these names the people would vote to remove them. Most people never knew they were Confederate Generals. And it took until 2020 to put potentially in place a ban of the Confederate Battle flag from all military facilities. Why not also discharge those who flew the flag? They are not Americans. And do not belong in the military. This has been going on for 160 years. We need to end it.

Those who fly the Confederate flag to honor the Confederate view on white supremacy. This country was never a white only country. Remember the Indians? White people were a minority from the very beginning. These people and their relatives made it a white majority by reducing the population of other races. America is not the homeland of white people. This is just propaganda.

We have dealt with these issues long enough. Confederate dead are not Americans. This myth has been going on since Abraham Lincoln's time. We ended the war without any consequences to those who fought against American troops. We gave them back their guns to hunt and sent them home. These people rioted and pillaged, ignored new laws protecting the black population, lynched blacks, created the KKK, and stuck a finger in the eye of the federal government. They should have been shot on site. No trials. They got their second shot as citizens, and this is how they abused it? I guess the Republican party of Lincoln were more interested in making money from southerners than fixing a very broken problem.

Many black people have wanted reparations for slavery and the economic conditions since slavery. I agree, but I have a problem with who they want it from. I do not think it should be the United States government. I believe they should be the former states of the confederacy and those who proudly fly the confederate flag. Families of former slaves now live in all 50 states. The collection should be by the federal government and distributed to all these families. Family history would need to be submitted to receive the funds. White families who had children with slaves need to pay additional reparation for them as well.

Let us fix this problem NOW.

COMPROMISE

This has become a dirty word in politics. The far left and far right seem to think so. I guess they were the ones who took the ball and went home when they did not get their way as kids. Or got on the floor and threw a tantrum when they did not get what they wanted for dinner. I am not sure, but it does seem a little childish. Where are the adults in the room who can tell their base that this was the best they could get at this point? Without compromise and to explain yourself to the children in your base on their level, we will never get anywhere in this country. I first heard "My way or the highway" while living in Mississippi. It was wrong then and it is wrong now. It does not belong in politics. And a bit self-centered.

To bring this country together we need to bring back compromise and teach our base that getting 25 to 50% of what you wanted is how our democracy works. Insisting on 100% of what you want is wrong and un-American. A one-way approach is tantamount to having a king, dictator, or much worse. Compromise is a win/win for both sides. If your goal is just to win for your side, that is un-American. Both sides need to win. That is what America is all about. No one size fits all. This is not a football game. There should be no winners and losers.

SOCIALISM, ANARCHY, AND AUTHORITARIANISM

We have seen these governmental models on the far right and far left. It comes from a feeling that Democracy is not working for them and change is needed. Young people are very much pushing these changes. There is a lesson to learn for everyone over 40 years of age. Unless big changes are made, one of these three types of government will prevail.

I am so tired of the 1% running this country. Money should not dictate power. It destroys the one man one vote scenario. Why should I vote if the 1% runs the country? I think this is one reason for the low turnout in elections. It does not matter who wins, little will change. The people need to take back the government.

Another reason for Democracy not working is lobbying. When this country was new, it was a necessity. With little communication nationwide, lawmakers needed special interest groups to inform them on issues they knew little about. This is not true today. It has become more about influence peddling than providing information. There are more perks, money for campaigns, vacations, etc. that are offered to buy support for their ideas. The only lobbyists that should be allowed are the voters who put him or her in office. This needs to be fixed.

Another money issue against Democracy is the election donations. We have no idea who they are. It is all too secret. I can think of a lot of groups, individuals, and causes that voters might have a problem in support of their candidate. Voters need to know who is supporting each candidate. It can tell you more about what the candidate believes in and who. This must be fixed.

Another issue is lifetime politicians. The more time in office, the more corrupt they become. Whenever term limits come up in discussion, it is always said it is up to the states. The states say if they pass it, other states will not. And with seniority in congress being an issue for appointments to committees and chairman-ships and other leadership roles, this is a real problem. The only way it can change is by either Constitutional Amendment or Con-stitutional Convention. I do not recommend the second choice. But it needs to be fixed.

Why do we have an ancient system of voting in this country. Voting in person is old, very costly (voting machines are not cheap) and dangerous to foreign influence. Voting help volunteers are getting harder to get. The internet is not an answer currently. Very unsafe and unsecure. Voting by mail is the answer. Ballot counting machines are fast and accurate. If there is a challenge, you can count them by hand. We need a permanent fix for this problem.

We have made minor changes to our democracy over the last 200+ years. We need to get these done.

THE OBVIOUS TRUTH

Politicians and some journalists and talk radio hosts lie like an old hound dog. You cannot believe anything they say. It has become so rampant in one party. They lie to their party voters all the time. They assume they are stupid and will believe everything they say. As wrong as it is. They believe it or say they did not mean what they say. All of this is making fun of free speech. 200+ years ago I do not think they were writing this into law to protest blatant lies and liars. Just a different opinion.

Many politicians lie for their lobbying and donor friends. They do not want anyone to believe the truth. They want the voter to believe their point of view. Even if it goes against common sense.

To these people, anything they do not believe in are said to be said by liberals. In this pandemic, that means not taking care of the people. That is a liberal idea. But giving money to corporations, huge businesses or wall street is being American. Bull Shirt. These people pay politicians to do their dirty work. Ever wonder why most tax breaks go to the 1%? I will let you ask them that. But expect a lie. They do it so well.

You must always ask yourself who is behind a movement for or against a law. Let us take one example—The Affordable Care Act. Most people love it. Insurance companies, the rich, anti-abortionists/religious right, and some medical specialists do not. Follow the money. These groups and individuals are making campaign donations. They want to go back to the way it used to be. Any politician who says this law is bad is getting or wanting to get donations from them. The next time you do not vote, remember this. They will.

Media groups who continually lie need to be taken off the air or boycotted by advertisers. Enough is enough.

Why do we never say anything back to them when they lie or say bad things about reporters at a press conference. Are you afraid you will not be asked back to the next one? Who cares? People do not want to hear from liars. Get derogatory. Call them a bad word or name. They deserve it.

I look forward to the day when people run for congress not expecting to make money. Politicians will not fix this problem. You the people will need to demand it.

QANON

I have researched this group and find it very alarming. Some have said that this group was created by an anonymous Q that is American, is a Trump supporter, and has grown to 3 million followers. They are extremely right wing, white supremacist, believe in the deep state wanting to take down Trump, and that Democrats and lefties are trafficking children or worse yet, eating them. They are also Evangelical. There are a lot worse they believe in, but at the moment let us stick to these areas.

Why are these people believing these things. They are scared of change for one thing. They want the life of white people in the 1950's. They also believe in making laws based on biblical teachings. Not the rule of law. They believe in gods law and the mandate that god rule this country. They are the worst side of Evangelicalism. They don't believe that Democrats and Liberals are Americans because they don't fit into their vision of America. They think Democrats and Liberals are evil. This movement needs to be eliminated.

REPUBLICAN PARTY IN 2020

There is a lot to fix here, but there are going to be a lot of inter-party fighting. If the party is ever going to be in power again, they are going to have to change their base and some of its principles.

Republican politicians tell their own base lies. They know the base will believe anything they say. And their lies are backed by Fox News (that's a joke--news, really?) All the other networks are owned by American corporations. Fox news was owned by a foreigner until his death, and displays his view of the world. Do you really think Fox News is the only network that tells the truth? Now that idea is a big joke.

You as a member of the base need to ask politicians in the republican party the hard questions. Make them back up what they say with evidence and facts. If they don't have a basis for what they are saying or their answer smells like rotting fish, call them out on it. Don't forget, they work for you. Not the other way around.

There are parts of this base that turn off the general public. Neo Nazis, White Supremacists, Qanon, Militias, and those who want to walk around everywhere wearing or carrying a gun. Lets look at these groups one at a time.

Neo Nazis are the plague I thought we got rid of in WWII. My dad fought to get rid of it fighting in Europe. But they were Nazis, not Neo Nazis. You know, the real thing, Not little boys running around with big mouths big guns and flags. What did the Jews or any other group do to you? Get real. Nothing.

White Supremacists have been with us since before the Civil War. It is a problem in this country since the birth of this country. If England had Black Kings, the revolutionary war would have been much earlier in our history. The idea that white people must be in charge of this country is bull shirt. Change is coming. Not to your benefit, but it is coming.

I have talked about Qanon earlier in this book. It is the worst side of Evangelical Christian faith. They use their faith as justification for their crimes. Do you remember the Qanon member who killed a person at a Pizza restaurant? Enough said.

Militias were allowed early on in this country because many people did not trust big government not to become dictators or kings. Also, to replace a standing army. It was a way to appease the wary. States had militias, and they became the National Guard. It is the Independent Militias that have lost their way. They support the things that they were supposed to be against.

To those of deep faith. The laws you want passed are not good for this country. Lets look at a few you helped pass. Your ban on Alcohol in the 1920's was the best thing for organized crime in this country. Citizens died in the gang wars. Reminds me of the War on Drugs. Same thing. When this country had a ban on Abortion prior to Roe-V-Wade we witnessed the death of Women and Children. You can't dictate Morality. Win it with common sense and truth. Not lies.

The vast majority of Americans are tired of the same issues you haved pushed for decades. Low taxes for the rich and high taxes for the middle class, smaller government which means the end to Social Security, Medicare, Food Stamps and Medicaid. And lets not forget racism and backing law enforcement. Anti-Abortion also needs to realize that abortion is here to stay. All these issues have already been decided by most Americans. And not in your favor.

Gun violence is at an all time high with military assault weapons. America is tired of your lack of response. You wait for the NRA for guidance. You work for the NRA and not the people. The second Amendment does NOT protect your right to semi-automatic rifles. It protects one shot rifles and pistols. That is all.

Our country is badly broken. We need to look ahead. Not back. The answers we seek look into the future. It will take a long time before the voting public trusts the Republican party after Donald Trump. You need to fix your base.

RIOTING AND RACISM

The rioting about police shooting and killing Black members of the community who are unarmed. A tragedy. Martin Luther King lived in the 1960's. The country today does not look or feel like the 1960's. He was a man of faith. I am not sure his approach to non-violence is the right idea today. You have been rioting and speaking for decades. You have been lambs for the slaughter because you did not meet violence with violence. No one is going to give what you want unless you fight for it. Yes, some black people will die as in all wars. You are in a war. But black people are already dying. What is your point? We have an Amendment to the constitution called the second amendment. You can own and use guns. You just need to buy one and get a permit. If there had been a man with a gun in the crowd of people standing by watching black men be killed, the four officers in Minneapolis would be dead, not George Floyd. The reason they are not afraid of you when they kill another black man is the words of MLK. They no you will not bear arms and fight. Let the older generation live by his words of non-violence. You are going to have to take out as many white supremacists as you can. Look what is going on. Take your multicolored glasses off and see. Younger people are joining the white supremacist movement. The young man who killed all those people in El Paso, TX was in his early 20's. The gunman in Wisconsin was a militia member and 17 years old. And had an assault rifle. Where is yours? Meet violence with violence. Why has no group in the black community stood up and fought for black rights? You can shoot a white supremacist and disappear into the black community. And by the way, don't forget their families. Even little Janey is going to grow up in an environment of hate. So kill her, too. This is a war. Dyllan Root on death row will be alive for decades. He was only 21 when he called for a race war. How many of these young people are going to come out of the wood-work and kill black people.

Forget justice. It has failed you all your lives. Even if the officers are convicted, Donald Trump will just parden them. Don't forget the biggest biggot in the country lives in the White House. One day even Donald and his family must pay the price. You can't forget anybody. Many of you have military training. Use it to train the others. This has been going on for over 200 years. Be the gen-eration to stop it. Those whites in the black lives matter move-ment. Get involved. This war will never end unless you take up arms. Not all police are bad. But the ones who kill unarmed blacks must die. Only kill those and their families.

I know the older generation will not accept what I say is true, but you must convince them that cowing down to White Suprema-cists and waiting for justice has not worked. You need another path.

When the civil rights movement of the sixties transpired there were not open in public deaths of black people. They did not want the media attyention. White Supremacists have become more bold and want media attention. They are daring you to kill them in public. After killing 2 and wounding 1 our 17 year old in Wisconsin was smiling. You need to smile when you kill his White Supremacist family. Every one of them.Last time I checked he was still a minor. His parents are responsible for his actions. Make it so.

Protesting non-violently is a very good idea. What you need to do is shoot looters and those causing damage in our cities. Rioters. Not your people. They are trying to make you look bad. Take care of the problem. Don't wait for others to fix the problem. They won't.

I guess what I am saying is----Do you want to be laid to rest as sheep or as a fighter if you get killed. I am not really for vigilantism. But in this case I am. Fight as if your life depended on it. Because it does. The only way to change over 200 years of White Supremacy is good violence. You need to stop sitting on the sideline as the next one to die might be you.

Electing Biden is just the first step. But he will not stand with you. He's a politician and has to worry about voters. But what he is saying will take decades to change. How many black people will die in the meantime. Biden says changing sustemic racism that lasted for over 200 years will take time. Why are Neo-Nazi's, White Supremacists and private Militia not on the list of known domestic terrorists. And why is Qanon running for congress. Gee, how about the Taliban? Congress should not seat any Qanon members selected for congress. Unless they denounce it as false and fake. Ask every politician that question. Some will say that they have a right to free speach. Somehow, I do not think the founding fathers wanted to protect these groups. If hate is a free speech, then it is time to change the constitution.

This is the younger generations war. Fight it or live with the consequences. The country needs you to act. Do so.

FOOD STAMPS

Food stamps or SNAP feeds America's poor people and children. Now that being said they say it is a state run program. Maybe that is why I received over $100.00 a month in Florida and $15.00 a month in Tennessee. This program is underfinanced and needs help. The guidelines are not relevant for today. They need serious rethinking and redoing. I only make $896.00 a month on disability. But in Tennessee I make plenty of money to buy groceries, pay rent on section 8 and utilities. I don't think so.

I have spent my entire life working since I was 15 years old. Non stop since my strokes in 2010. I have taught school, managed restaurants and ran my own business and this is what I get? The country should be ashamed. I have finally become comfortable with being poor. That is what I am. I have seen both sides of the spectrum.

Mark my words. If you make a great living, and it all ends tomorrow with a disability, how are YOU going to pay for anything the rest of your life. Lets just hope you are over 60, because it is based on what you already paid into Social Security. Not like me in my early 50's. Welcome to poverty. I guess you are only as poor as you feel. Until the bills come due. Disability does NOT turn off the bills. You owe less, but you also make less.

POLITICAL PARTIES

Political parties have been around since Washinton and Jeffer-son's time. Washington was opposed to the idea of parties and Jefferson was for it. In his final address to the American people, Washington warned that political parties would divide the nation. He definitely got that right. Look at these two parties today. So polarized they could not agree if it was a day of sunshine or rain. One party wants to set up a committee to investigate the matter and the other wants to condemn their findings. Like anything else, just look outside. It is actually overcast.

Parties get caught in the weeds over getting re-elected and what their donors and support groups want. The sad truth is that political parties seldom support their voters. Or they support the overal views of the far right and far left. And we people in the center just decided which candidate is the better of two evils. Neither is perfect.

We have gotten to the point where we don't compromise and support getting 100% of what we want and 0% of what the other party wants. This is why so little gets done in Washington. The people don't nominate the candidate they want. The party faithful do. The consequences can be grave. When Biden did not run in 2016 the party nominated Hillary Clinton. The East and West coast and women in the rest of the country were thrilled. The first woman president. Forgetting that polls showed a severe divide in this country over reality (successful Senator and Secretary of State) and her list of bad acts as the first lady. People don't forget. Hillary Clinton is the reason Donald Trump won the whitehouse.

No candidate stepped up to the plate that year. Where were all the women who ran for President this year in 2016? Yes, I do blame blind trust for a candidate who was so flawed that Donald Trump won. I knew she would not win regardless of who the Republicans nominated. Or what they said. To name just a few issues, not divorcing her husband after an affair in the White House. I do not know how you feel, but as a man, I was flabborgasted. As women, you forgave her? Men would not. She liked the power of being in the white house as first lady. And would not give it up.

 Lets not forget the scandels. Travel Gate, and others. But let's not forget the taking of white house property when they moved out. If someone had not said something, they would have gotten away with it. They appolizied and returned the items, but most Americans were not sure if this was not done on purpose. Gifts to presidents are gifts to the people. Not to the individual.

 In essence, the Democratic party screwed up. And they should never forget this incident in history. Not just Donald Trump getting elected but how the Democrats failed the country. You can't get around it.

 Republicans need to realize that you ran 16 candidates in the primary, and got Donald Trump. You got into the party when it meant something. The party has changed. You have denied what the party has become for a decade. Now you can't. In 2012 you put together a plan to recruit minorities into the party. And guess what, the base rejected it. They want a White Supremacy party. After Trump, you can stand on the house or Senate floor and becry what is going on, but expect to be laughed at because you blindly supported Trump. The OLD Republican party will never return with this base. You need a new base. Or start your own party.

We could open up the system and allow independents to run on the same balanced field as the two major parties and debate in this country. This would drastically reduce the stranglehold of the two party system. It is very unfair today. We need to change it.

IN CONCLUSION

We are a country of hope and confidence. In believing that we can do better. We need change.

ABOUT THE AUTHOR

John Donovan

Who Am I? I am a 62-year-old man, soon to turn 63, with two college degrees and a lot of life experience. I am also in a wheelchair from strokes since 2010. I was once a Republican up until after the George H. W. Bush Presidency. The party was changing, and in my opinion not for  the better. There were those who were in denial about the groups in their base. All you had to do was listen to the base of the party. I got sick of it and left the Republican party.